On Undue Influence

A Forensic Psychology Primer

Book One of the Forensic
Psychology Primer Series

Max Wachtel, Ph.D.

CHERRY
CREEK
PRESS

BOOKS BY MAX WACHTEL, PH.D.

The One Rule For Boys

Sociopaths & Psychopaths

Narcissists & Narcissistic Personality Disorder

On Undue Influence

Library of Congress Cataloging-in-
Publication Data
Names: Wachtel, Ph.D., Max, author
Title: On Undue Influence: A Forensic
Psychology Primer / Max Wachtel, Ph.D.
Description: [Denver, Colorado]: Cherry Creek
Press, [2024] | Includes footnoted references.
Identifiers: LCCN 2024922967
ISBN 978-0-9988783-6-2 (paperback)

This book is a work of nonfiction. Any
references to real people and events have been
obtained from publicly and readily available
information sources, and names and pertinent
details have been changed/excluded to protect
those persons' anonymity.

www.maxwachtel.com

Contents

For Kim and the kids

Introduction

Chapter 1: The curious case of the Doe family[1]

Juan and Cordelia Doe lived on 10,000 acres of profitable ranchland in a rural county in the United States. They tried their hardest to treat their two daughters, Flora and Amber, equally. Cordelia was so concerned about this that she obsessed

---

[1] The case of the Doe family is based on a real undue influence case. I did not work on this case, but the details are in the public record. I have changed the names of all involved, and I have also changed key details to maintain anonymity. However, the major facts of the case remain unchanged.

over making sure each child received the exact same amount of candy at Christmas. At one point, the Does gave one grandchild a $5,000 loan. When that grandchild did not pay back the loan, Juan and Cordelia gave each of the other grandchildren $5,000 to make up for the discrepancy.

In 1980, Juan and Cordelia executed wills that gave their money and property to one another upon the other's death. If both died at the same time, Flora and Amber were to share equally in their inheritance. Juan died in 1993, and Cordelia inherited his estate. In 2002, at the age of 87, Cordelia executed a Last Will and Testament that disinherited Flora completely and left her entire estate to Amber. In 2004, she executed a codicil to her will, essentially an addendum, which continued to disinherit Flora.

As you might imagine, Flora was not pleased.

In 2006, upon Cordelia's passing, Flora contested the 2002 Will and 2004 Codicil, claiming Cordelia lacked testamentary capacity and further alleging Amber unduly influenced their mother.

And let the fight begin.

Although testamentary capacity and undue influence are related, they are different legal concepts and require a different analysis by experts. Testamentary capacity deals with whether people executing an estate plan know what they are doing and are competent to make the decision about who will inherit their money after they die. When thinking of all the different types of legal capacity (e.g., medical decision making, contractual capacity, competency to stand trial, etc.), testamentary capacity is at the bottom of the capacity pile: it requires the lowest level of capacity to clear the legal hurdle, and thus, it is often difficult to prove a person did not have testamentary capacity.

Undue influence is different. In every state, it only takes a simple majority of the evidence to prove an individual unduly influenced the testator, or the person who executed the will.

Since that is the case, most claims of testamentary incapacity are often coupled with claims of undue influence. Incapacity is extremely difficult to prove. Undue influence is often the disinherited family member's last, best shot at nullifying a will or an estate plan. It is still difficult to prove, but it is often the only legal route available for a person who thinks they are entitled to money from an estate.

Back to the Doe family. Here is what we know about their situation (*remember, I was not involved in this case and have no inside information. I have gathered all the information about this case from publicly available sources*):

Amber was a registered nurse, and she moved to the ranch to care for her aging parents in 1989. After Juan died in 1993, Amber remained at the ranch to care for Cordelia, who had numerous health issues. In 1997,

Cordelia, who was 82 at the time, was kicked in the head by one of her cows and suffered a significant brain injury. She required a multi-week hospital stay and never fully recovered. In fact, she developed a speaking problem related to the head injury that kept her from expressing herself with more than one or two words at a time.

The sisters, Amber and Flora, teamed up to care for their mother after her head injury. Amber focused on providing full-time, live-in care to her mother, and Flora managed Cordelia's finances.

In exchange for their help, Cordelia allowed Amber to possess the south half of the ranch rent free and receive a monthly stipend. Flora leased the north half of the ranch for a below-market rate. Flora wisely subleased her portion of the ranch for more money than she paid, and she kept the excess money in a special account for Cordelia's future care.

Early in 2002, Amber, still living with her mother, told Flora she wanted the northern half of the ranch too, which would have enabled her to control the entire ranch. Flora did not go along with this plan initially, and Amber dropped the issue. By August of that year, she again told Flora she wanted the whole ranch, saying Cordelia wanted it that way.

Amber then wrote a lease termination letter that she said Cordelia signed, kicking Flora off the land. Flora countered by immediately filing an emergency petition for appointment of a temporary conservator for Cordelia. A conservator is a court-appointed person, either a family member or a professional, who manages the money for a person who cannot manage their money on their own.

As the animosity between the sisters increased, Amber hired attorneys for her mother, communicated with them, and read their letters to Cordelia. Amber told everyone her mother was upset about the conservatorship and the lease dispute. At the eventual trial, evidence came out that it was Amber, not Cordelia, who was upset with Flora. Amber also kept Flora from visiting the ranch and communicating with their mother.

Amber hired an estate planning attorney late in 2002 to write

Flora out of Cordelia's will; she said her mother wanted this to happen. Amber communicated extensively with the estate planning attorney and explained all the reasons why she, Amber, did not like her sister. Without speaking to his client, the estate planning attorney wrote up the proposed will, just like Amber wanted him to do, and brought it to Cordelia to sign. Amber explained to the attorney that she wanted to do whatever it took to keep Cordelia's money from going to "the wrong side."

Cordelia's conservatorship attorneys got word of what Amber had done and thought the new will would be invalidated if challenged. They met with Cordelia, conducted a lawyerly evaluation of her testamentary capacity, and executed a

second will later in 2002. This will
still kept Flora from inheriting any
money or property from the estate.

During this whole process, an
independent nurse who conducted a
home visit expressed concern that
Amber was isolating Cordelia from
Flora.

Cordelia passed away in the
spring of 2006, and a probate of her
estate was opened. Flora challenged
the validity of the 2002 will (and a
subsequent codicil from 2004) on the
grounds of lack of testamentary
capacity and undue influence on the
part of Amber.

The state circuit court
invalidated the 2002 will and 2004
codicil. The Court found that Cordelia did, in fact, have testamentary
capacity but that the will and

codicil were the product of undue influence.

Amber appealed the decision to the state's Supreme Court, who affirmed the circuit court's ruling. The points they felt strongly indicated undue influence were as follows:

1. Amber had a confidential relationship with her mother;
2. Amber controlled who had access to her mother;
3. Amber prevented Flora from communicating with Cordelia;
4. Amber contacted the attorneys and told them what was to be in the 2002 Will;
5. Amber was instrumental in dealing with the estate planning attorneys;

6. Amber arranged the witnesses to the will signing to be present;

7. Cordelia was susceptible to undue influence;

8. Amber had the opportunity to exert undue influence;

9. Amber was predisposed to exert undue influence over her mother, evident from persistent efforts to gain control and possession of Cordelia's property; *and*

10. There was a clear result that benefitted Amber to the detriment of her sister; under the terms of the 2002 will and 2004 codicil, Amber's inheritance increased by several million dollars, and Flora's inheritance dropped to zero.

Although in all states, the standard of proof for undue influence is a preponderance of the evidence, it remains a difficult concept to prove. Every testator, to some extent, is influenced by others, but it is almost never an *undue* amount of influence. It is not until the testator's free will is destroyed and they are compelled to make changes to their estate plan they would not have otherwise made that influence is considered to be *undue*. Further, even when undue influence *has* occurred, it is almost always done in secret, leaving little evidence of nefarious activity. You almost never see a case where a live-in caretaker is on video saying, "If you don't give me all your money, I'm going to stop feeding you."

Regardless of the difficulty in proving undue influence in general, Flora was able to provide enough circumstantial evidence to the state circuit court to convince it that Amber had unduly influenced their mother. Flora and her astute attorneys followed their state's standard for proving undue influence, which includes the elements of (1) a decedent's susceptibility to undue influence, (2) an opportunity to exert undue influence and effect wrongful purpose, (3) a disposition to exert undue influence for an improper purpose, and (4) a result showing the effects of such undue influence. In that state, if you can prove all four elements by a mere majority of the evidence, you have proven undue influence occurred.

And in the case of Cordelia Doe, both the circuit court and the Supreme Court agreed that Cordelia had testamentary capacity. Despite her significant head injury, Cordelia was able to leap over that low hurdle. The courts ruled Cordelia knew what she was doing when she wrote her daughter, Flora, out of the will. The problem was that the will was the product of undue influence by Cordelia's other daughter, Amber; Cordelia would not have written Flora out of her will without the extreme pressure from Amber.

Amber's actions are a textbook example of undue influence. What is unusual about the curious case of the Doe Family was that there was so much evidence against her. That is not typically the case, which makes undue influence difficult to prove.

And that is my job: knowing what to look for to prove or disprove claims of undue influence in an objective manner. Further, that is what I aim to do in this book: point out those elements and how to evaluate them.

My goal is to provide useful information to both attorneys and non-attorneys about a niche and esoteric aspect of estate law and forensic psychology. Many attorneys I have worked with already know everything I will cover in these pages, but I have discovered through my work that there are also many estate planners and litigators who have not had much direct experience prosecuting or defending an undue influence case. This is not a dig at those attorneys; this is an emerging field, and many attorneys, even those who have been practicing for decades, have yet to run across it in their practice.

With that in mind, my hope is that attorneys find the information in this book to be useful, whether it is brand new to them or whether they are well versed in undue influence case law and theory. And, I cover some very basic areas of law that every attorney is sure to know (e.g., burden of proof, level of evidence needed, differences between various types of evidence). For non-attorneys, my hope is that this basic information will make the concepts in the book more comprehensible.

For attorneys, this book might help you understand how you can use an expert to strengthen your case. For forensic psychologists, you might discover an area of practice most psychologists have never thought about. For everyone else, you might discern something interesting about human nature. Everyone might glean some useful tips to protect their elderly loved ones.

I will examine the legal concepts that dictate the elements of undue influence, and I will use the Doe case to explain how forensic experts tie psychological principles to those legal concepts to form opinions in a real-life undue influence setting.

Before I get too much further, I also want to point out that the Does are real people. Their family struggles are real, and they fought a real case in court that had a real impact on their lives and the lives of many others. At the end of the case, the details of their lives were published as case law, and all that information is on the Internet for the whole world to read.

That is the reality of undue influence cases. They involve human suffering, abuse, neglect, and a host of negative emotions. Typically, these families have had a long history of strife, and instead of grieving the loss of a loved one, they take their family strife public. One side always wins the legal case, but it never feels like a true victory.

Let's try to keep that in mind when we learn more about Amber and Flora Doe. We don't know the pain they've been through. We don't know what caused their animosity toward one another. We don't know their struggle. We only know a few of the

worst possible facts about them. They
are full human beings, with all the
good and all the bad that comes with
that.

With that in mind, let's begin.

Next up: Allow me to introduce
myself.

Chapter 2: Allow me to introduce myself

If you haven't already gathered this information from the cover of this book, my name is Max Wachtel. I am a forensic psychologist. People think I have the coolest job in the world, and they're right.

It is a common misconception that forensic psychologists work with the FBI or police departments to profile individuals and catch criminals. Those important professsionals are behavioral profilers or behavioral analysts. Rather, the American Psychological Association defines forensic psychology as "the application of psychological principles and techniques to situations involving the civil and criminal legal system.[2]"

Translating that into friendlier terminology, forensic psychologists evaluate individuals to help attorneys, judges, and juries answer legal questions that have a psychological bent to them. For example, is a mass murderer legally insane? Is a defendant capable of working with their attorney to assist in their defense? Are there aspects from the bank robber's life that help explain why they did what they did?

---

[2] VandenBos, G. R. (ed.). (2015). *APA Dictionary of Psychology* (2nd ed.). Washington, D.C.: American Psychological Association.

Those are all questions forensic psychologists are trained to answer. They take their specialized knowledge and training in psychology and apply that knowledge and training to the legal issues on which they are asked to form opinions.

I got my start in forensic psychology working on criminal cases. Since 2004, I have conducted more than 2,000 evaluations. I've met with shoplifters and first-degree murderers. Drug addicts and psychopaths. I've worked in 46 different prisons and jails, including the ADX Supermax: the federal prison in Florence, Colorado that houses Al Qaeda members and the Unabomber (before he passed away). I am one of a handful of civilians who was granted a full tour of the Supermax, and I'm not allowed to talk about it in detail. Let me just say two things: it is completely underground, and it is impossible to break out of.

Although I still do criminal forensic work, many years ago my practice shifted. In roughly 2012 I started conducting evaluations for probate court (called chancery court or orphans court in various states). I work with elderly individuals who may need a guardian or a conservator. I have completed hundreds of neurocognitive evaluations and have seen every type of dementia you can imagine, including one very rare type that causes frequent urinary tract infections as one of its main symptoms.

Unlike most professional mental health practitioners, many of the clients I evaluate are no longer living.

Like Flora Doe, there are a lot of would-be heirs who believe their deceased loved one was taken advantage of when they executed their will. In fact, there's a whole industry built around it. Estate litigators who sue or defend those who have been sued. Certified Public Accountants who look through bank statements. Private investigators who scour social media. Handwriting analysts who determine whether grandma's signature on the will was a forgery. And forensic psychologists, who piece together medical records, correspondence, estate planning documentation, and witness statements to form opinions on testamentary capacity and undue influence.

That last one, that's me. I've worked on cases where people fought over $50,000. I've worked on cases where people fought over $4.5 billion. I have worked on a case where an elected official scammed multiple people, including her own brother, out of a relative's inheritance (people lost jobs over that case). I worked on one case where scammers posed for photos with a dead body to prove how close they were to the deceased.

At this point in my career, I have conducted undue influence evaluations all over the country, and I have studied and written on undue influence statutes and case law in all 50 states.

I don't take every undue influence case I am offered. And I tell every attorney who hires me that they may not like what I have to say after I analyze the data. I will not stretch the evidence. I will not ignore inconvenient facts. I will not put myself in a position where I have to justify a bad expert opinion in a deposition or at trial. But when I feel confident in my analysis and opinions, I write a strong report that is simple to defend.

I document everything I do as objectively as I can (presuming it will eventually become available for opposing counsel and other experts to review), and I never worry about giving an attorney bad news and not getting hired again. I am far enough along in my career that I know new referrals will come my way. I am also far enough along in my career that I know opposing counsel often reaches out to me after the conclusion of the current matter to hire me for their new cases.

One last thing about me: I was a university professor for twelve years, where I taught classes in psychological and neuropsychological assessment and in the ethical and legal practice of psychology. For those of you who are keeping track, it took me 21 years to leave college.

One *last* last thing about me: I am not an attorney. I know a lot about a very specific type of law, and I write extensively about legal concepts in this book. But I am not an attorney. I am a licensed psychologist, and I can practice psychology in states where I am licensed or credentialed. I cannot practice law anywhere. I have specialized know-

ledge experience, training and
education in undue influence law,[3]
and I have testified as an expert in
both the legal and psychological
aspects of undue influence. Further,
in order to do their jobs properly
forensic psychologists must understand the legal concepts on which
they are opining. But please don't
construe anything in this book as
legal advice. I promise my des-
criptions of undue influence laws and
other legal concepts are accurate,
but if you have a legal question or
want legal advice, don't ask me. Ask
an attorney.

---

[3] See Federal Rules of Evidence, Rule 702.

Chapter 3: Definitions

I'll keep this chapter short. You might be tempted to skip it, and I don't blame you. Most people don't sit down and read the dictionary. I promise I will only share a few definitions, but they are important. It will help you understand the terminology I use throughout the rest of the book.

1. _Burden of Proof_: "The necessity or duty of affirmatively proving a fact or facts in dispute on an issue raised between the parties

in a cause.[4]" Also, the side that has the responsibility of proving something in court. As in, "I think Grandpa's caretaker unduly influenced him. I have the burden of proving that to the court. If I can't prove it with the required amount of evidence, the court must find that no undue influence occurred."

2. *Codicil*: "A testamentary disposition subsequent to a will, and by which the will is altered, explained, added to, subtracted from, or confirmed…but not revoked.[5]"

3. *Circumstantial Evidence*: I don't want to spoil the surprise. For a

---

[4] Black's Law Dictionary. Retrieved from www.thelawdictionary.org.
[5] *Id.*

full description of this term, see Chapter 12.

4. *Confidential Relationship*: I don't want to spoil the surprise. For a full description of this term, see Chapter 5.

5. *Decedent*: The person in the legal case who died. As in, "Grandpa, the decedent, died and left all his money to charity."

6. *Direct Evidence*: I don't want to spoil the surprise. For a full description of this term, see Chapter 12.

7. *Estate*: The personal belongings, money, and real estate owned by someone. As in, "Grandpa's estate consisted of $100,000 in cash, two houses, and a collection of cars."

8. *Heirs*: The people who stand to inherit money from someone. As in,

"Grandpa left me $10,000 in his will. I am one of his heirs."

9. *Natural Heirs*: The people who would inherit money from someone if that someone died without a valid will. These are typically children, grandchildren, or other family members. As in, "Grandpa's adult children are his natural heirs. They will inherit all his money unless he writes a will that says otherwise." Natural heirs are sometimes antiquely referred to as *natural objects of one's bounty*, which makes them sound like pirates.

10. *Preponderance of Evidence*: More than half of evidence in a legal case. As in, "51 percent of the evidence demonstrated that Grandpa was unduly influenced.

That is a preponderance of evidence presented to the Court."

11. *Property*: Anything contained in the estate. As in, "Grandpa's property consisted of $100,000 in cash, two houses, and a collection of cars."

12. *Testator*: A person who makes a will. As in, "Grandpa became a testator when he went to his attorney's office and signed his new will."

13. *Undue Influencer*: The ne'er-do-well who forces the testator into doing something with their estate that they wouldn't otherwise do. As in, "The caretaker was an undue influencer because they convinced Grandpa to leave all his money to them."

PART 1: Legal concepts underlying undue influence

Chapter 4: What undue influence is

Every state has a slightly different definition for *undue influence*. The Uniform Probate Code, a guide for states to use if they choose, does not define the concept. Most states have not codified a definition into their probate statutes, either. The definition for *undue influence* in each state must be pieced together from case law and civil jury instructions.

Regardless, most states use a similar definition; in fact, the definitions are similar enough that I feel comfortable sharing what my research has concluded to be a common definition for undue influence amongst all 50 states and the District of Columbia.

First, a quick point: not all influence is undue. For example, it is okay for a spouse to influence another spouse's testamentary decisions. It is also okay for a child to influence their parent's decisions, and vice versa. Influence is okay, and I would argue, unavoidable.

Undue influence is different, and it is not okay.

Essentially, every state has the following two legal elements that must be present for *influence* to turn into *undue influence*:

1. Undue influence must destroy the testator's free agency; *and*
2. Undue influence must cause the testator to make their estate plan, or any part of their estate plan, different than they otherwise would have if there had been no undue influence.

Let me parse those elements out a bit so they make more sense.

First, the undue influence must destroy the testator's free agency. Many states use that exact language in their case law on undue influence. Other states write that undue influence must cause a person to lose their free will when they are preparing and executing their estate plan. They both mean the same thing. I personally like the *free agency* language better because it can be confusing to distinguish between *will* (a "voluntary choice or decision"[6]) and *will* ("a legal declaration of a person's wishes regarding the disposal of [their] property or estate after death"[7]). Take it from me, it's tough to write clearly about a person's will in making their will and determining if their will was of their own will.

Anyway, language aside, free agency and free will tend to be used interchangeably in the context of undue influence. And, undue influence must cause a person to lose their free agency, meaning their

---

[6] Merriam Webster. (2020). *Merriam Webster's Collegiate Dictionary* (11th ed.). Faridabad, India: Author.
[7] *Id.*

decisions are not a voluntary choice on their part.

Second, undue influence must cause a person to make any part of their estate plan different than they otherwise would have. So, Grandma has lost her free agency and her decisions are not her voluntary choice; if her testamentary decisions led her to distribute her property in ways she would not have done had she not been influenced, then the legal criteria for *undue influence* has been met and a court must nullify the estate plan on those grounds.

Let me give you an example. Grandma has several adult children. One child has convinced Grandma to leave all her money to charity because it is the noble thing to do. Grandma has a history of giving most of her money to charity. Even though she might want to leave her estate to her adult children, there's a decent chance she would have left her money to charity anyway. Although Grandma's adult children might be upset, this is probably not undue influence. Grandma's free agency *might* have been destroyed by the child, but Grandma *probably* would have left a lot of her money to charity anyway; the adult child's influence did not cause Grandma to act in a way she would not have done had it not been for that influence.

Contrast that to a situation where an adult child convinces Grandma to leave her entire estate to that child, forsaking Grandma's other children. Grandma feels pressure to acquiesce because the influencing child has been her care giver for years, and she does not want to lose this child's support; if she does, she will be all alone in her remaining years. She has a well-documented history of treating all her children equally (remember Cordelia Doe from Chapter 1; Cordelia was so steadfast in her equality she made sure each of her children received the same amount of candy). Grandma makes the non-voluntary decision to give all her money to the influencing child, which she would not have done had it not been for that child's influence. That is *undue* influence.

To summarize: Influence is okay. Influence that causes a person to make non-voluntary decisions they otherwise would not have made is not okay.

It's simple. Shouldn't that be the end of the book?

I wish that were the case. The fact of the matter is that nothing is as simple as it seems with psychology or the law, and undue influence is no different. Although the basic legal definition for *undue influence* is relatively straightforward, there are myriad nuances that keep estate litigators and people like me busy.

For example, some states require that there be some sort of negative outcome for a potential heir in order for influence to be undue. If the adult child from the above example was Grandma's only child and that adult child forced Grandma to make the non-voluntary choice to leave her estate to charity rather than give it to the only child, even though Grandma would not have made that non-voluntary decision but for the child's influence, there is no negative outcome for one of Grandma's natural heirs. The money would have gone only to the adult child, and that child didn't want it.

Other states do not require a negative outcome for influence to be undue. In the above example, it may be that the adult child's child (aka the grandchild of Grandma) might complain. In that case, if this scenario had taken place in a state that does not require a negative outcome for the heir, the grandchild might prevail and force their parent to take Grandma's money, which may eventually become the grandchild's money.

So yes, undue influence is both simple and extremely nuanced and complex. I'll keep writing. You decide whether you want to keep reading.

Next up: What is a confidential relationship, and why is it important in undue influence cases?

Chapter 5: A confidential relationship is not what you think it is

In every state, a relationship based on authority and power must essentially exist between the decedent and the undue influencer in order for undue influence to have occurred. Without that type of relationship existing, the undue influencer would typically not have the opportunity to unduly influence the testator. Many times, the power/authority relationship is considered *confidential*. When most people hear *confidential*, they think *secret*. Most of the time, they are correct. We all have secret, confidential relationships with our doctors, our accountants, our attorneys, and our clergy. Those professionals are bound by law to keep what we tell them secret, with a few limited exceptions.

In the context of undue influence, a confidential relationship is something very different from what I described above. Although *secret* may be part of the relationship, that is not its defining feature.

Rather, a *confidential relationship* in undue influence cases is one where one party has justifiably reposed trust and confidence in another party. Instead of being a *secret* relationship, it is more of a *trusting* relationship.

Generally speaking, if a person gains the trust and confidence of another person by acting (or pretending to act) for the benefit of or in the interest of the other person, then a confidential relationship exists. For example, if your family member acts in your best interest (or fakes it really well), you will likely start to trust them. This is the beginning of a *confidential relationship*.

Beyond developing trust, your family member may be put into a position to exercise influence and control over you. For example, if you trust your family member so much that you give them $1,000 to take to the bank and deposit on your behalf, that family member now has some amount of power over you. A key to the legal concept of a confidential relationship is that it must be a trusting relationship where there is a power imbalance.

An easy way to think about whether a confidential relationship exists is whether you relax your care and vigilance in your relationship with the other person more than you would with a stranger. Going back to the bank example, if you would give your family member $1,000 to deposit in your account but you would not give a random stranger off the street that $1,000 to deposit, you might have a confidential relationship with your family member.

Confidential relationships might arise if one party has taken steps to induce another party to believe that they can safely rely on the first party's judgment or advice. For example, "You can trust me. I work with money all the time. Give me the $1,000 and I'll deposit it in the bank for you before I go to the grocery store."

One sticking point: in order for a relationship to be confidential, the trust and confidence must be *justified*. If you give $1,000 to your family member, who you know to be an upstanding citizen, your trust in your family member is justified. If you give $1,000 to a bank robber, you can't claim you had a confidential relationship with the crook after he steals your money.

One other sticking point: in order for a relationship to be confidential, the person you are reposing confidence in must accept your trust. If you try to foist $1,000 on a family member who tells you repeatedly that they are untrustworthy and you should not trust them yet you insist, you can't claim that relationship was confidential when your self-admitted untrustworthy family member loses your money.

The takeaway is this: It is a threshold legal condition that a relationship of authority and power (often a confidential relationship) between the testator and the undue influencer must be established and proven as a matter of fact before it is even possible to adjudicate the question of whether undue influence occurred. Although it is more complicated than this, if there is no confidential relationship, then it is extremely difficult to prove undue influence. After all, if you don't trust someone or believe they have your best interest at heart, they couldn't possibly influence you to do something you wouldn't otherwise do (unless there is coercion or force involved).

Next up: What undue influence isn't.

Chapter 6: What undue influence isn't

At this point, we know that a relationship based on authority and power (sometimes deemed a confidential relationship) must exist between the influencer and the person being influenced. We also know that undue influence must destroy the testator's free agency, and it must cause the testator to make all or part of their estate plan differently than they otherwise would have.

We also know that not all influence is undue. Sometimes it's just influence.

For example, in most (but not all) situations, spouses cannot unduly influence one another. That's typically just called influence. Your spouse of 30 years can tell you they will stop talking to you if you cut your children out of the will. That's not typically undue influence.

However, recent spouses are likely able to unduly influence a testator. Imagine a situation where an 80-year-old man marries a 37-year-old woman who used to be his caretaker, and he leaves his entire estate to her, cutting out his children from his first marriage. The new spouse may not have engaged in undue influence, but it sure looks suspicious.

The normal pressure family members put on testators to add something or take something out of a will is not undue influence, typically. Making suggestions about what should or should not be in a will is not undue influence, either.

Undue influence cannot occur without the opportunity to influence: if a charity was made the sole beneficiary of the will but they did not learn about the testator's largesse until after the testator died, the charity necessarily could not have unduly influenced the testator. Although a third party may have influenced the testator to give their money to the charity (see Chapters 14 and 15 for more information on this type of situation), the charity just never had the opportunity to do so. Also, as mentioned in the last chapter, if the potential influencer had no power or authority over the testator, they probably did not have the opportunity to exert undue influence.

Undue influence also does not typically occur if there is no motive to influence: if a long-lost relative ends up inheriting the testator's estate but that long lost relative didn't know the testator, has a good job, and has never needed money from others, it is hard to say that long lost relative had a motive to unduly influence the testator.

So, typically, motive and opportunity are necessary conditions to prove undue influence. However, almost every jurisdiction in the United States recognizes that motive and opportunity alone do not mean undue influence occurred.

Also, most jurisdictions recognize that influence from a friend or family member that is based on love, affection, or kindness is not undue influence. If a caretaker is shown to have been extremely kind to the testator over the course of the last 15 years of the testator's life, and the caretaker tells the influencer, "You know, I love your classic car. My dad had one just like it. You should think about giving it to me," that is right on the threshold, but it may not be undue influence (obviously, an evaluator would need to look at many other factors in this case to form a solid opinion; for example, maybe the testator had always wanted to give that car to their grandchild and they feel threatened by the caretaker, which would point away from love and kindness and toward undue influence).

It is important to note that not all jurisdictions think this way. In some states, love, affection, and kindness are seen as a type of manipulation that undue influencers might use to destroy the testator's free agency. A few jurisdictions list 'performing or withholding sex acts' as a specific form of manipulation that can lead to undue influence.

Finally, just because a testator's estate planning decisions do not sound proper or fair or right, that doesn't mean they're due to undue influence. Sometimes, people are jerks, and they are allowed to be jerks with their money. Just because Mom left all her money to her youngest child, forsaking her other children, that doesn't mean the youngest child unduly influenced Mom. Mom's decision sounds mean. It sounds unfair. It will almost certainly lead to a lot of family strife after Mom passes away. But she has the right to make that mean, unfair decision, presuming she is of sound mind and has not otherwise been unduly influenced.

Next up: Does it matter if the undue influencer received a gift while the testator was still alive?

Chapter 7: The difference between wills and *inter vivos* gifts

A will gives instructions regarding how a testator's estate should be divided after the testator dies. An *inter vivos* gift, on the other hand, is a gift given to a person while the testator is still alive. In fact, *inter vivos* literally means "between the living" in Latin.

In most states, case law is clear that testamentary distributions after death and *inter vivos* gifts while still alive are treated the same regarding the issue of undue influence. An influencer can just as easily force a person to leave them something in their will or force them to give up property while they are alive. From a psychological perspective (which we will get to soon), it doesn't matter when the gift or property is transferred; the underlying processes are the same.

Some states, however, put more scrutiny on *inter vivos* gifts than they do testamentary instructions. There are two reasons for this.

First, a will is inherently changeable until the testator dies, but *inter vivos* gifts almost always are not. An example: Grandma decides to write a will leaving her estate to her heirs in equal parts. Ten years later, several of her heirs have angered her, so she executes a new will leaving out those pesky heirs. Two years later, Grandma and the pesky heirs reconcile, and she puts them back in the will. Several months later, Grandma passes away, and her heirs inherit her property in equal shares.

In that same situation, if Grandma had decided to give each of her heirs $1 million at the same time she executed her first will, she can't get that money back when, ten years later, several of her heirs became pesky. The *inter vivos* gift transactions have already occurred, and she no longer owns that money.

This is a reason why some states focus more on the issue of undue influence when *inter vivos* gifts are challenged. Since a will can be changed, a potentially greedy undue influencer takes a risk by convincing a testator to give them their estate after they die. It is much safer to unduly influence the person to give them the money now.

A second reason why some states focus more heavily on *inter vivos* gifts is related to the first: these gifts immediately deprive the person of the use of the gifted property. If Grandpa gives away his home while he is still alive, he no longer has free use of that home (there are certain situations where there may be a legal agreement that Grandpa gets to live in the home for the rest of his life even though he no longer owns it, but you get my larger point). If Grandpa proposed to give his home away after he dies, he still has free use of his home for the rest of his life, regardless of whether someone unduly influenced him to give them his home in his will.

Even in states where the case law is less clear, most courts understand that they must take seriously any gift that immediately deprives a person of the use of their property (*i.e.*, an *inter vivos* gift), especially when a petitioner has raised the issue of undue influence.

Next up: What does the field of psychology have to say about undue influence?

PART 2: Psychological theories of undue influence

Chapter 8: The SODR model

The SODR model of undue influence[8] contains the following elements:

1. Susceptibility to undue influence;

2. Opportunity for the influencer to exert undue influence;

3. Disposition of the influencer is such that they may be likely to engage in undue influence; and

---

[8] American Law Institute. (1999–2023). Restatement of the Law (3d) of Property—Wills and Other Donative Transfers. Philadelphia, PA: Author; § 8.3, comment e.

4. <u>Resulting</u> transfers or estate plans appear to be the effect of undue influence.

On the surface, these four elements are relatively common sense and straightforward. Applying them to specific cases is not as easy as it seems, however. For example, how do you determine if a testator is susceptible to undue influence? What is a disposition for undue influence? What type of transfer gives the appearance of undue influence?

In Chapter 11, I will cover in detail how psychologists determine susceptibility to undue influence.

Disposition toward undue influence is a tricky topic. At first blush, it sounds as though the expert psychologist needs to evaluate and make judgments about a potential influencer's personality style that would lead them to be willing to scam the elderly. That is a harsh judgment to make about a person the expert psychologist has likely never met, seen, or even talked to.

In fact, the American Psychological Association (APA) Code of Ethics,[9] Rule 9.01(b) indicates, "Psychologists provide opinions of the psychological characteristics of individuals only after they have conducted an examination of the individuals adequate to support their statements or conclusions."

On first reading, this code makes it sound as though a psych-

---

[9] American Psychological Association (APA). 2017. *Ethical Principles of Psychologists and Code of Conduct* (2002, amended effective June 1, 2010, and January 1, 2017). Washington, D.C.: Author.

ologist cannot make evaluative statements about a person if they have not met with the person individually. However, that is not actually the case. Note that Rule 9.01(b) states psychologists provide opinions only after an examination of the individual that is *adequate* to support their statements or conclusions. There are situations where an expert psychologist conducting an undue influence evaluation will have enough direct and circumstantial evidence about the potential influencer (sometimes including the potential influencer's own words through their written and oral testimony) to be able to adequately comment on their disposition.

The APA Code of Ethics even allows for this situation in Rule

9.01(c), which indicates there are times when an in-person evaluation is not necessary. In such cases, the psychologist must explain "the sources of information on which they based their conclusions and recommendations.[10]"

So, it is possible for undue influence experts to comment on the potential influencer's disposition, as long as the following conditions are met:

1. There is enough evidence to justify such comments;

2. The evaluator explains they did not personally evaluate the potential influencer; and

---

[10] *Id.*

3. The evaluator is clear on what sources of information they used to make their comments.

Although it is often possible to form an opinion on the disposition of the potential influencer toward or away from undue influence, there is still the question of what type of disposition might lead a person to unduly influence another person.

Disposition can be defined as "the dominant quality or qualities distinguishing a person,[11]" and a person's "prevailing tendency, mood, or inclination.[12]" And, a person's tendencies, moods, and inclinations are most accurately gleaned from an examination of their past behavior,

---

[11] Merriam Webster (2020).
[12] *Id.*

which is often discovered through a thorough review of records (e.g., bank records showing large transfers, actions that lead to isolation of the vulnerable adult, threats made via email or voicemail).

A person's personality structure certainly adds to their disposition, and personality structure is not easily gleaned from a records review only (unless that records review includes previous psychological evaluations). Typically, an in-person evaluation is necessary to accurately comment upon a person's personality.

When I conduct undue influence evaluations using the SODR model, I do not comment on the potential influencer's personality (unless I have a previous psychological evaluation on which to rely). I comment on their documented actions and other life factors in my assessment of their disposition toward undue influence. Commenting on their personality without adequate evidence is a violation of the APA Ethics Code. Further, it is unnecessary and unhelpful. A classic book from 1968 indicates that, although important, personality factors account for less than 10% of our behavior.[13] Avoiding making evaluative judgments about a potential undue influencer's personality structure is in keeping with the APA Ethics Code and good science.

---

[13] Mischel, W. 1968. *Personality and Assessment*. Hoboken, NJ: John Wiley & Sons.

There are numerous behavioral and situation-based clues that might lead a forensic evaluator to conclude that a potential influencer has the disposition of an undue influencer. Although not an exhaustive list, here are some common factors evaluators look for in their analyses:

1. What type of relationship the influencer and the testator have (e.g., family member, paid care giver, attorney);

2. The financial, emotional, and legal stability of the influencer (e.g., declared bankruptcy three times, in and out of jail, emotionally unstable);

3. How involved the influencer was in the preparation of the will (e.g., found the attorney, made all

the appointments, reviewed drafts, attended the will signing);

4. Actions the influencer took to isolate the testator (e.g., changed a phone number, moved the testator out of state, monitored visits with friends and family);

5. Indications that the influencer took advantage of the testator while the testator was alive (e.g., received large gifts of money, was included on bank accounts, became the testator's financial power of attorney); and

6. Any other suspicious activity on the part of the influencer.

The flipside of having a disposition toward undue influence is, of course, having a disposition away from undue influence. Maybe the person accused of undue influence donates large sums of money to charity, encourages the testator to go to their longtime attorney and work individually with that attorney to create a new will, and is independently wealthy. It is important to look for factors that might lead an evaluator to conclude that, although a potential influencer had the opportunity to influence and benefitted from the provisions of the will, that potential influencer did not have a motive or the overall behavioral disposition toward undue influence.

Once you have determined susceptibility, opportunity, and disposition in the SODR model, it is time to determine if the resulting estate plan or property transfers have the appearance of undue influence. This is a tricky endeavor, because not all suspicious looking estate plans, deeds, or money transfers are the product of undue influence.

Some transfers can, on their face, appear to be improper or unfair. Writing a child out of a will sounds cruel and unfair. Giving 50% of one's money to a care giver sounds improper. But, maybe the disinherited child is in prison, or maybe the care giver in question has lived with and cared for the testator for the last 25 years. Or, maybe the testator is just mean to their kids. Although unfair, that does not constitute undue influence.

When undue influence evaluators look for resulting estate plans or transfers that give the appearance of undue influence, they are looking for circumstances that are outrageous. For example, a care giver who has only known the testator for 6 months might not deserve 50% of the estate. Or, a child who had been set to receive their inheritance in a series of wills starting 50 years ago but was written out of the will within 6 months of the testator dying might indicate the potential for undue influence. It is up to the evaluator to determine, through the careful review of evidence, what the testator's longstanding testamentary wishes were and if there were any rational reasons for making changes to that longstanding plan, especially given the timing of the estate plan change (e.g., was it done shortly before the person died; whether any

new beneficiaries were added or any
longtime beneficiaries removed, etc.).

And that is the SODR Model.
Next up: What do undue influencers
have in common with stalkers, sex
assaulters, and domestic abusers?

Chapter 9: Stalkers, sex assaulters, domestic abusers, and undue influencers? Really?

This is a touchy subject, and accusing someone of acting like a stalker or a sex assaulter can be highly offensive and inappropriate. Nevertheless, research from Brandl, Heisler, & Stiegel (2008)[14] highlighted

---

[14] Brandl, B., Heisler, C. J., & Stiegel, L. A. (2008). The Parallels Between Undue Influence, Domestic Violence, Stalking, and Sexual Assault. *Journal of Elder Abuse and Neglect (17)3.*

some of the commonalities between undue influencers and perpetrators of domestic violence, stalkers, and sexual assaulters in terms of their tactics and severity (e.g. grooming victims, ongoing relationships, stealthy actions by influencers, financial exploitation, influencers being charming, influencers justifying their actions through excuses, victims sometimes appearing as willing participants, and victims often experiencing trauma reactions).

Brandl, et al. highlighted the following potential actions taken by undue influencers:

1. Keeping the victim unaware of the influencer's true intent;

2. Isolating the victim from people and/or information;

3. Creating fear in the victim;
4. Preying on vulnerabilities in the victim;
5. Creating dependency in the victim on the influencer;
6. Encouraging a lack of faith in the victim's abilities;
7. Inducing shame and/or secrecy in the victim; *and*
8. Engaging in intermittent acts of kindness.

Aside from the provocative statement that undue influencers and stalkers, sex assaulters, and perpetrators of domestic violence have a lot in common, the Brandl Model can be a useful framework for understanding some of the potential actions and tactics undue influencers use to get their way and to destroy the free agency of their victims.

This model is most useful when the amount of coercion needed to overcome the testator's free agency is high. If all it takes to "coerce" a testator into signing a new will that goes against their wishes is to place the piece of paper in front of them and ask them to sign it, the Brandl actions are not necessary. But when the testator is more cautious and functioning at a higher level, Brandl's model fits; undue influencers need to work harder to get the testator to bend to their wishes, and they often employ some or all the above-mentioned actions.

Next up: The IDEAL Model

Chapter 10: The IDEAL model

Bennett Blum's IDEAL model of undue influence, which has been published and/or cited by the American Bar Association's Commission on Law and Aging, the American Psychological Association, and the National College of Probate Judges,[15] indicates the following factors are related to undue influ-

---

[15] Retrieved from www.bennettblummd.com/undue_influence_ideal_model.html

ence, all five of which are necessary for undue influence to have occurred:

1. Isolation, referring to "isolation from pertinent information, friends, relatives, or usual advisors;[16]"

2. Dependency, referring to "dependence upon the perpetrator, such as for physical support, emotional factors, or information;[17]"

3. Emotional Manipulation or Exploitation of a weakness, which "often manifests as a combination of promises and threats regarding either issues of safety and security, or companionship and friendship. Perpetrators

---

[16] *Id.*
[17] *Id.*

sometimes make use of victim weakness or vulnerabilities;[18]"

4. _Acquiescence_, referring to "the victim's apparent consent or submission. The act is not truly voluntary, but is instead the product of inaccurate, misleading or deceptive information that is believed due to the victim's impairments and/or relationship with the perpetrator;[19]" and

5. _Loss_, referring to "damages, such as inter vivos financial loss.[20]"

Blum's IDEAL Model is straightforward, with two important twists. First, most undue influence researchers talk of _isolation_ in terms of being isolated from other

---

[18] _Id._
[19] _Id._
[20] _Id._

people, such as family, friends, and trusted advisors. Blum adds isolation from information into the mix, which makes sense. For example, if an undue influencer is keeping the testator from receiving mail, phone calls, and emails, it is likely the testator is missing pertinent information that might otherwise help them resist the undue influencer's coercive actions.

Next, Blum points out it can sometimes look like the testator was acting of their own free will when, in fact, they had been unduly influenced. I have worked on cases where an elderly person insists they had not been manipulated; they really wanted to give that online scammer $100,000. Sometimes, a testator is acting of their own free will and making unfair or seemingly improper decisions. Other times, they have been unduly influenced. It is up to the expert evaluator to properly and thoroughly review all the available evidence to determine, if possible, if the testator's seeming acquiescence was autonomous or the product of excessive coercion.

Next up: Tying it all together with the California Undue Influence Screening Tool.

Chapter 11: Tying it all together: The California Undue Influence Screening Tool (CUIST)

In the late 2000s and early 2010s, a nurse and advocate for the elderly named Mary Joy Quinn evaluated previous models of undue influence and found four common features. Her work has been published in multiple peer-reviewed publications,[21,22] and it is, by far, the best tool for undue influence experts to use when determining whether undue influence has occurred.

The four common features that often indicate undue influence has occurred are as follows:

1. The elderly individual's susceptibility to undue influence;

2. The authority or position of power a potential influencer has over the elderly individual;

3. The actions taken or tactics used by a potential influencer to gain

---

[21] American Bar Association/American Psychological Association (2008). *Assessment of Older Adults With Diminished Capacity: A Handbook for Psychologists.*
[22] Quinn, M. J. (2010). Undue Influence: Definitions and Applications. A Project Supported by the Borchard Foundation Center on Law and Aging.

control over the elderly individual; and

4. Any unfair or improper outcomes to the elderly individual's emotional, physical, or financial health because of the potential influencer's actions or tactics.

Quinn did not stop there. Through further research, she and colleagues determined there were numerous subfactors for each of her four common features that can be objectively measured to better understand whether undue influence has occurred. These features and subfactors are all contained in the California Undue Influence Screening Tool (CUIST).[23] Quinn, et al.

---

[23] Quinn, M. J., Nerenberg, L., Navarro, A. E., & Wilber, K. H. (2017). Developing an Undue Influence Screening Tool for Adult Protective

initially developed the CUIST as a tool for Adult Protective Services workers to determine if further investigation would need to be taken or if law enforcement would need to get involved due to the high potential for financial exploitation or undue influence of the elderly adult in question. It is equally useful in retrospective evaluations of undue influence when the elderly adult in question is deceased (and, its factors and subfactors are general enough

---

Services. *Journal of Elder Abuse & Neglect, 29*(2-3).

that it applies in every state, not just California).[24,25,26,27]

I won't list them all in this book, but Quinn and her colleagues identified fourteen subfactors for assessing the testator's susceptibility to undue influence, fourteen potential actions or tactics undue influencers may have used, and eleven potential outcomes that would in-

---

[24] Greene, A.J. (2023). Elder Abuse and Violence: Undue Influence and Vital Decision-Making Capacities. In Martin, C.R., Preedy, V.R., & Patel, V.B. (Eds), *Handbook of Anger, Aggression, and Violence* (pp.1141-1161). New York, NY: Springer.

[25] Milton, J.C., & Guzman, K.R. (2019). Decision and Persuasion: Re-Conceiving the Role of the Planner Where Undue Influence is Suspected. *ACTEC Law Journal, 44*(1).

[26] Nerenberg, L. (2019). *Undue Influence in Policy and Practice Handout*. From the Enhanced Multidisciplinary Team Conference of the Upstate Elder Abuse Center, Lifespan, and the Well Cornell Medicine/New York City Elder Abuse Center, September 18, 2019.

[27] Bownes, E.M. (2023). *Attorney Perspectives of Financial Capacity Among Older Adults*. Doctoral Dissertation, University of Alabama.

dicate undue influence likely occurred. The CUIST is thorough, and when used properly, it can clearly demonstrate the likelihood (or lack thereof) of undue influence having occurred in any given case.

One word of warning: The CUIST was designed with California undue influence and exploitation laws in mind. Although similar, every state has slightly different criteria. It is important for undue influence experts to be aware of the definitions and regulations in the jurisdiction in which they are working and understand that certain aspects of the CUIST may not apply (or that one or two extra subfactors might need to be added to the CUIST to fully account for the jurisdiction in question).

Next up: How undue influence is proven.

PART 3: How undue influence is proven

Chapter 12: A quick detour to explain the difference between direct and circumstantial evidence

When people are evaluating the strength of another person's argument, they will sometimes say, "Your argument is just circumstantial," as though that is a criticism of the quality of the argument. Regardless of the strength of the argument in those situations, building a legal case through circumstantial evidence is not necessarily bad. In fact, I would argue that some forms of circumstantial evidence are stronger than some forms of direct evidence. Further, every state allows for undue influence cases to be proven largely through circumstantial evidence, because direct evidence in undue influence cases almost never exists.

This, of course, begs the question: What's the difference?

Black's Law Dictionary[28] defines *direct evidence* as "the proof and testimony that directly go to an issue at hand." It further states, "When the existence of any fact is attested by witnesses, as having come under the cognizance of their senses, or is stated in documents, the gen-

---

[28] Retrieved from www.thelawdictionary.org.

uineness and veracity of which there seems no reason to question, the evidence is said to be direct or positive."

The same dictionary defines _circumstantial evidence_ as "evidence directed to the attending circumstances; evidence which inferentially proves the principal fact by establishing a condition of surrounding and limiting circumstances, whose existence is a premise from which the existence of the principal fact may be concluded by necessary laws of reasoning." It further states that when "the existence of the principal fact is only inferred from one or more circumstances which have been established directly, the evidence is said to be circumstantial."

You gotta love legal writing.

Let me give you a common example of direct versus circumstantial evidence so it makes more sense: Did it snow last night?

Let's say there is a court case that hinges on whether it snowed last night. You are the key witness. At 11:30 P.M., you looked out your window and saw snow falling from the sky. When you testify under oath about what you saw, that is direct evidence (*i.e.,* it is something you directly witnessed through one of your senses). Case closed. You saved the day with your direct evidence.

Now, let's alter the scenario. You were exhausted last night, so you went to bed at 9:00 P.M. You looked out your window and saw it was not snowing (a piece of direct evidence). You woke up at 6:00 A.M. the next morning, looked out the window, and saw there was a foot of snow on the ground (another piece of direct evidence). These two circumstances (that you witnessed no snow at 9:00 P.M. and that you witnessed snow on the ground at 6:00 A.M.) led you to infer, through the necessary laws of reasoning using surrounding and limiting circumstances, that it snowed last night. Case closed. You saved the day with your circumstantial evidence.

In this case, which type of evidence is better? Most would argue either direct evidence or circumstantial evidence used to prove it snowed last night are equal. Neither is more or less helpful for the jury.

There is, however, a general belief amongst the public that direct evidence always trumps circumstantial evidence. I caution that this is not the case. For example, psychologists have known for decades that eyewitness testimony is highly unreliable; humans are terrible at remembering situations and events accurately. Yet, eyewitness testimony is direct evidence. In cases that hinge on eyewitness testimony, attorneys often have more success convincing juries that something did or did not happen through expertly crafted circumstantial evidence that appeals to the jury's innate sense of logic.

I raise this issue in a book on undue influence because there is almost never direct evidence proving someone unduly influenced someone else. By its very nature, undue influence is done in secret, away from prying eyes. Rarely is there a case where an undue influencer tells someone else their scheme, James Bond villain-style, and on camera.

Instead, undue influence cases are typically built on circumstantial evidence. This is so well accepted in the field of elder law and estate litigation that almost every state has case law stating as much. In order to prove (or disprove) undue influence, circumstantial evidence leading to logical inferences is necessary, and there needs to be a decent amount of it.

Next up: Shifting burdens of proof and the amount of proof needed.

Chapter 13: Shifting burdens of proof and the amount of proof needed

If you remember from your thorough study of the definitions in Chapter 3, the <u>burden of proof</u> refers to the duty of proving facts in dispute on the main issue raised in court.[29] In the context of this book, the main issue raised in court is whether undue influence occurred.

---

[29] *Id.*

One party has the duty of proving undue influence occurred. To do that, they must prove the disputed facts lean in favor of undue influence having occurred.

This is like the prosecuting attorney in a criminal case having the duty to prove the defendant is guilty. In a criminal case, there are a lot of facts in evidence. Some of those facts are undisputed. Many, however, are disputed. For example, it will be an undisputed fact that the police were able to find fingerprints at the scene. No one will argue against (or dispute) that fact, and fingerprints at the scene of the crime are direct evidence. But, the prosecution and defense will attempt to convince the jury that the fingerprints mean something vastly different. The prosecution may attempt to argue that the fingerprints match those of the defendant (if proven, this is more direct evidence), and the fact that the defendant's fingerprints are at the scene mean the defendant committed the crime (circumstantial evidence). The defense may try to argue that, since there were fingerprints for seven different people found at the scene (direct evidence), there is no way of knowing which of those seven people committed the crime (circumstantial evidence, raising doubt in the jury's mind).

In a criminal trial, the prosecution has the burden of proving the defendant committed the crime, and it must be proven _beyond a reasonable doubt_, which federal courts define as "proof that leaves you firmly convinced the defendant is guilty. It is not required that the [prosecution] prove guilty beyond all possible doubt. A reasonable doubt is a doubt based upon reason and common sense and is not based purely on speculation. It may arise from a careful and impartial consideration of all the evidence, or from lack of evidence.[30]"

Will the prosecution in this case be able to use the circumstantial evidence of the defendant's finger-prints at the scene to add to the evidence they argue proves guilt beyond a reasonable doubt? Will the defense be able to raise enough

---

[30] District Courts of the Ninth Circuit. (2021). *Manual of Model Criminal Jury Instructions.* See § 3.5: Reasonable Doubt—Defined.

reasonable doubt about the fingerprints to cause the jury to disregard
that evidence? I don't know. But,
that's how the burden of proof and
the amount of proof needed works at
a criminal trial.

In a civil or probate trial,
which is where undue influence cases
are heard, the burden of proof and
the amount of proof necessary is
different from criminal trials. Let's
start with amount of proof necessary
first, since that is the easier part
to both write about and understand.

In every state in the United
States, the side which has the burden
of proof (ignore which side that is
for a minute) has the duty to prove
undue influence occurred or that
undue influence did not occur by a
preponderance of the evidence. This

is the evidentiary standard where
"the burden of proof is met when the
party with the burden convinces the
fact finder that there is a greater
than 50% chance that the claim is
true.[31]"

In an undue influence case,
there can be a lot of doubt in the
Court's mind about whether undue
influence occurred, and the Court
still might decide that at least 50%
of the evidence points to undue
influence. That is the nature of a
civil case: 49.9% percent of the
evidence can point away from undue
influence, but the Court can still
find that undue influence occurred

---

[31] Definition from the Legal Information
Institute at Cornell Law School. Retrieved from
www.law.cornell.edu.

and use that finding to invalidate a gift or a will.

Random aside: In most situations, undue influence trials are bench trials: a trial heard by a judge only, and the judge decides the verdict. There are nuances to this, including how the case is filed, but that is too far afield for this book. For our purposes, you should presume undue influence cases are decided by a judge (aka the Court) and not a jury.

So, the Court must decide if there is a preponderance of direct and circumstantial evidence that points to undue influence or lack of undue influence. It's a low standard.

Now, who has the burden of proof in an undue influence case? That answer is not so simple.

When the case starts, the side petitioning the Court to invalidate a gift or a will based on undue influence has the burden of proof. That side is often referred to as the Petitioner. The Petitioner in an undue influence case needs to accuse a specific someone of undue influence. That specific someone is often referred to as the Respondent. Think of the Petitioner like the prosecutor in a criminal case, and the Respondent is like the defendant accused of a crime.

When the case starts, the Petitioner has the burden of proof. But, that burden can shift. Intrigue!

If the Petitioner can prove to the Court that the Respondent was in a confidential relationship with the testator *and* that the Respondent had some hand in preparing the new will or effecting the gift, then the burden shifts to the Respondent.

But, that burden can shift back to the Petitioner. What?! More Intrigue!

I should mention that, in a few states, the burden does not shift back. And, in a few states, all that is needed is proving a confidential relationship existed to shift the burden (it doesn't matter if the Respondent had any role in changing the will or making the gift). But, in most states, the burden shifts back to the Petitioner when the Respondent demonstrates there is some evidence that any actions they took were in good faith and that there is doubt that undue influence occurred.

The process I described is called a shifting burden. In undue influence cases, the burden often shifts back and forth, but in most states it almost always ultimately lands on the side of the Petitioner having to prove undue influence occurred by a preponderance of the evidence.

If the Petitioner demonstrates to the Court that there was a confidential relationship and the Respondent took actions to alter a will or have the decedent make a gift to them, and the Respondent does not provide a response, the Court must find that undue influence occurred (not in every state, but this is how it works in most states).

If the Respondent responds to the Petitioner's allegation with even a minimal amount of evidence demonstrating good faith and a lack of undue influence, that is typically enough for the Court to say the Respondent has met their burden, and the burden then shifts back to the Petitioner (again, not in every state, but in most states).

There is often legal wrangling back and forth regarding who has the burden of proof. If you can imagine, both sides want *the other side* to have the burden because it is typically easier to defend something than it is to prove something in court. The long and the short of it, however, is that in almost every case, the burden ends up resting with the Petitioner, the person accusing the supposed ne'er-do-well of undue influence.

Next up: When can a non-beneficiary be an undue influencer?

Chapter 14: When a non-beneficiary can be an undue influencer

Typically, the person who benefits from the undue influence (the beneficiary) is the one accused of undue influence. If a father, on his deathbed, signs a will disinheriting three of his four children, then the remaining child is the beneficiary, and they might be accused of undue influence.

But let's say the child who remains in the will was estranged from his father and hadn't seen or spoken to him in years. That child was out of the country when the father signed the will and did not even know their father was sick. It will be almost impossible for the other children to prove that the estranged child engaged in undue influence.

But let's say there's a nefarious stepchild involved. Intrigue!

This stepchild hates their stepfather's biological children. They want to sow discord and make everyone angry. To do this, they hatch a plan to convince the father, as he is dying and in his weakened mental and physical state, to write all the children out of the will, except for the estranged son. Muaw hah hah hah!

There is a preponderance of evidence that the stepchild engaged in undue influence to overpower their stepfather's free agency and convince him to change his will in a way he would not have otherwise done without their interference. They are the undue influencer. But, other than getting satisfaction out of watching their plan come to fruition, they did not benefit at all from the provisions in the new will.

Can the stepchild really be an undue influencer? Can the will be thrown out on the grounds of undue influence?

In this case, probably. The proof is so extreme and the outcome is so unfair that a Court would likely invalidate the will and have all the kids inherit equally from their father's estate.

But, what if the facts are less clear (maybe more in the 50-50 range) and the alleged undue influencer is the testator's attorney or another professional like a CPA? Can an estate planning attorney be an undue influencer if they are offering what they believe to be sound legal advice to their client?

Maybe. Maybe not. It depends on the state. In a few states, an essential element of undue influence is that the alleged influencer must have benefitted from the new estate plan in some way. Most states don't have that provision, though.

So, yes, it is possible in most states for a non-beneficiary to cause a will or a gift to be invalidated due to undue influence. However, it is difficult to prove that, especially when the accused influencer is a professional who isn't getting anything out of the deal (other than their customary fees, which they would get no matter the will's provisions).

In my experience, I have only seen one case succeed when a Petitioner alleged a non-beneficiary unduly influenced the testator for the benefit of someone else. I suppose it could happen again.

Up Next: Putting together the legal case.

Chapter 15: Putting together the legal case

I'll keep this chapter short since I am not a lawyer. Please do not construe anything in this chapter (or in the rest of the book for that matter) to be legal advice. Rather, I will share what I have gleaned from working on hundreds of undue influence cases and watching good attorneys put together good cases, even if those cases ultimately ended up failing at trial.

First, most undue influence legal cases also involve other legal arguments that have nothing to do with undue influence. For example, I have worked on cases where, in addition to undue influence being alleged, there are also allegations that a will or trust is invalid because the testator did not follow the legal requirements for executing a valid estate plan (e.g., the will was not witnessed by two outside observers, or the will was not notarized properly). In a sizable number of cases, the side contesting the estate plan will claim that the signature on the will was forged, and a handwriting expert will be hired to form opinions on that matter. In cases involving transfers of real estate, real estate attorneys might be hired to determine if the transfers were legal and valid.

In cases where multiple problems are alleged, it is important for the undue influence expert to avoid forming opinions on the issues that are outside the scope of their expertise. In cases where both testamentary incapacity and undue influence are alleged, I can conduct an evaluation and comment on both issues, since both are part of my expertise. But, I cannot comment on the validity of a signature or whether the will comports with the law in other ways. I have no better idea than anyone else if certain real estate transactions are legal.

The rest of this brief chapter will focus solely on how attorneys appear to put together the legal case for or against undue influence, but please know that is only a small portion of the larger legal case attorneys must build.

First, attorneys often look for a common set of suspicious circumstances when they are attempting to decide whether to take the case.

In the Restatement (Third) of Property (Wills & Donative Transfers),[32] the authors state there is no one exhaustive list of potential circumstances that suggest undue influence occurred. But, they did highlight eight common suspicious circumstances to help guide attorneys. Here is the list (which is a direct quote from § 8.3, comment h):

---

[32] American Law Institute. (1999–2023). Restatement of the Law (3d) of Property—Wills and Other Donative Transfers. Philadelphia, PA: Author.

1. The extent to which the donor was in a weakened condition, physically, mentally, or both, and therefore susceptible to undue influence.
2. The extent to which the alleged wrongdoer participated in the preparation or procurement of the will or will substitute.
3. Whether the donor received independent advice from an attorney or from other competent and disinterested advisors in preparing the will or will substitute.
4. Whether the will or will substitute was prepared in secrecy or in haste.
5. Whether the donor's attitude toward others had changed by

reason of his or her relationship with the wrongdoer.

6. Whether there is a decided discrepancy between a new and previous wills or will substitutes of the donor.

7. Whether there was a continuity of purpose running through former wills or will substitutes indicating a settled intent in the disposition of his or her property.

8. Whether the disposition of the property is such that a reasonable person would regard it as unnatural, unjust, or unfair.

Structuring the legal case for undue influence is, on the surface, relatively uncomplicated. Proving the case is much harder. But, this is essentially how a lawyer will structure an undue influence case:

1. The testator had a longstanding estate plan;

2. The testator was susceptible to undue influence because of [MAGIC TO BE EXPLAINED LATER!]

3. An undue influencer worked their way into the testator's life;

4. The undue influencer developed a confidential relationship with the testator;

5. The undue influencer had power and authority over the testator;

6. The undue influencer had the opportunity to exercise undue influence over the testator;

7. The undue influencer had a motive to exercise undue influence over the testator;

8. The undue influencer did bad things, as proven by [MAGIC TO BE EXPLAINED LATER!]

9. The undue influencer destroyed the testator's free agency and substituted their desires for the desires of the testator in newly executed estate planning documents; *and*

10. The resulting estate plan differed dramatically from the testator's longstanding estate planning wishes (as documented in bullet point #1).

11. There wasn't a reasonable or rational explanation for the estate planning change.

    THEREFORE,

12. Undue influence occurred.

To see how a case is put together, let's look back at the Doe case from Chapter 1 of this book. If you remember, Cordelia Doe, at the age of 87, executed a new will and a codicil to that will that disinherited her daughter Flora, leaving a large and valuable working ranch solely to her other daughter, Amber. Here's the general structure of a legal case from this real-life example:

1. The Doe parents had a long-standing estate plan. In 1980, the daughters were set to receive the ranch in a 50-50 split.

2. Cordelia, who was a widow since 1993, was susceptible to undue influence when she was 87 because [MAGIC TO BE EXPLAINED LATER!].

3. Amber, an RN, had lived with and cared for her parents since 1989.

She was a well-established part of Cordelia's everyday life.

4. Through her status as Cordelia's daughter, care giver, and everyday companion, Amber developed a confidential relationship with Cordelia, one where she had the ability to exert influence over her mother if she wanted to do so.

5. Because of this confidential relationship, and especially because she oversaw her mother's significant healthcare needs, Amber had power and authority over Cordelia.

6. Thus, Amber had the opportunity to exercise undue influence over her mother.

7. Presumably, Amber's motive for undue influence was money and/or control: she wanted the whole

ranch (note: it isn't essential to prove there was a motive to prove undue influence in the same way a prosecutor does not need to prove motive to prove a defendant is guilty of murder. But, being able to show there was a motive certainly helps).

8. Amber did bad things, as proven by [MAGIC TO BE EXPLAINED LATER!]

9. Amber destroyed Cordelia's free agency and substituted her own desires for Cordelia's desires, which is proven by the following:

   a. Amber ended up inheriting the entire ranch in the new estate plan, and Flora was written out of the will.

b. There was no good, explainable reason for Flora to be written out of the will. She had not had a falling out with her mother, she was not in prison, she did not do anything untoward, Cordelia had always wanted to treat her daughters equally, etc.

   THEREFORE,

10. Undue influence occurred.

At this point, you may have noticed that some magic happened in steps 2 and 8. Those are the hardest parts of a lawyer's legal case. How can a lawyer prove by a preponderance of the evidence that Cordelia Doe was susceptible to undue influence and that Amber did *something*

(or many *things)* that led Cordelia
Doe's free agency to be destroyed?

      Next up: This is where the
magic (to be explained now) happens.

Chapter 16: This is where the magic happens: Conducting the retrospective (*post hoc*) expert psychological undue influence evaluation

Let's get a few things out of the way first: 1) The Doe case is based heavily on the facts from a real, published case, 2) The Doe case has already been decided (the Court ruled that undue influence occurred), and 3) in a normal evaluation, an expert should go into the evaluation with no preconceived notion regarding whether undue influence occurred and should include specific evidence supporting their eventual unbiased opinion.

I already know the outcome of the case, so my analysis will be biased. It is my attempt to explain the possible reasons why the Court believed undue influence occurred and tie that reasoning to psychological theory. I will also try to point out any contradictory evidence that might point away from undue influence. I am not attempting to legitimize the Court's decision; if I had been hired as an expert in this case, my opinion may have differed from that of the Court.

With those caveats in mind, let's get to it.

Using the Quinn (2010) and
Quinn, et al. (2017) models, here is
what I get:

1. <u>Susceptibility to Undue Influ-ence</u>: Cordelia Doe was 82 years
old, and she suffered from a
traumatic brain injury from
which she never recovered. She
also had many physical health
issues. Cordelia was isolated from
others because of her health is-sues, and she was eventually
isolated from Flora, her daughter
who was written out of the will.
Cordelia was highly dependent on
others for help and care, as she
would not have been able to
survive without this help.
Cordelia had significant commu-nication problems and could
barely put two words together

(this is not an exaggeration; that was how witnesses described Cordelia's speaking ability). Plus, her condition was severe enough that potential influencers, especially those who knew her well, could have quickly spotted her vulnerability and exploited it had they wanted to. All these factors indicate Cordelia was highly susceptible to undue influence. This fact on its own, of course, does not prove undue influence occurred.

2. <u>The Authority and Power of the Potential Influencer</u>: This issue speaks to opportunity; did Amber, the accused influencer, have the opportunity to exert influence over Cordelia? The Court ruled Amber had a confidential rel-

ationship with her mother, meaning Cordelia trusted Amber, Amber either invited or accepted that trust, and she had power over her mother.

3. <u>Actions and Tactics of the Potential Influencer</u>: We know Amber had power and authority over her mother. But, did she use that power and authority in a way that is typical of undue influencers? Well, Amber moved into her mother's home and became her primary care giver. Amber started requesting more and more gifts from her mother, such as the ability to control all of Cordelia's property. Amber wrote a lease termination letter supposedly on Cordelia's behalf to try to kick Flora off her half of

the ranch. Amber hired the attorneys for Cordelia to fight Flora in court. Evidence demonstrated that Amber had ill will toward Flora, but Amber lied and said it was Cordelia who hated Flora. Amber also kept Cordelia isolated from Flora. Further, Amber hired the estate planning attorney who never talked to Cordelia but wrote the new will where Flora was disinherited after only consulting with Amber. These are all actions in which undue influencers engage to have their desires expressed in the person's estate plan rather than those of the testator.

4. <u>Unfair or Improper Outcomes</u>: An unfair provision in a will does not necessarily mean the testator

was unduly influenced. If a parent hates one of their children, they have the right to disinherit that child, even if that outcome seems unfair. However, it can be considered an improper outcome if a new estate plan differs dramatically from the testator's previous intent. This is where the Doe case is so strong. There was clear, demonstrable evidence that The Doe parents bent over backward to treat their children equally, at least monetarily (and from a candy standpoint). Several previous estate plans made it clear that Cordelia had not changed her mind on this issue: she wanted her two daughters to inherit equally from her estate. That, however, is not what happened in the 2002 will. In that will, Cordelia completely wrote Flora out of her half of the inheritance and everything went to Amber. Based on Cordelia's past wishes and the fact that there was no evidence Cordelia changed her mind about her testamentary intentions or her personal feelings toward her children, the provisions in the 2002 will were improper and unfair.

5. On the Other Hand: Cordelia's attorneys got wind of what Amber was doing, and they wanted to make sure Cordelia had the capacity to change her estate plan. They deemed Cordelia to have had the capacity to make her choices and that her choices reflected

Cordelia's true desires. This is evidence that points away from undue influence. The Court, however, did not think this evidence was enough to overcome all the evidence proving undue influence occurred in this case.

After the Quinn model, we move to the SODR model, and here are my thoughts:

1. Susceptibility: I already addressed this above. Regardless of whether undue influence occurred, Cordelia was highly susceptible to undue influence.

2. Opportunity: I already addressed this as well. It is clear Amber had the opportunity to unduly influence her mother, regardless of whether she acted on that opportunity.

3. Disposition of the Influencer:
   Without getting into what Amber's
   disposition or personality was,
   her behaviors strongly indicated
   she would be the type of person
   who would be willing to unduly
   influence someone else. For example, she lied and said Cordelia
   hated Flora when it was really
   Amber who hated Flora. Amber
   controlled who had access to her
   mother and cut Flora off
   completely. Amber contacted the
   estate attorney and dictated what
   she wanted in Cordelia's new will.
   Amber wrote legal documents in
   her mother's name that furthered
   Amber's desired outcome, not Cordelia's. Amber was persistent in
   her desire and efforts to control
   her mother's property while her

mother was still alive. All these
actions shout disposition toward
undue influence.

4. Resulting Outcome: As explained
   above, Cordelia's 2002 will gave
   the strong appearance of
   reflecting Amber's desires, not
   her mother's. In fact, the 2002
   will was an extreme departure
   from Cordelia's decades-long
   desire to have her daughters
   inherit her estate as equally as
   possible.

   Next up is the Brandl model:

1. Amber isolated Cordelia from Flora.

2. Amber preyed on Cordelia's vulnerabilities to get her to take
   actions and sign documents she
   likely would not have otherwise
   signed.

3. Amber <u>acted in her own self-interest</u>, using the authority Cordelia had given her. For example, Amber wrote a lease termination letter and sent it to Flora, and she hired attorneys to defend Cordelia against Flora trying to help her mother.

4. Amber created a situation where Cordelia was significantly <u>dependent</u> on her. Cordelia literally could not have survived without Amber. Counterpoint: Amber may not have created this dependence maliciously. There is no evidence Amber withheld medical care or food or medicine from Cordelia. Nevertheless, it's likely to have been in the back of Cordelia's mind that if she angered Amber, Amber might leave her.

5. Amber also likely <u>engaged in acts of kindness</u> toward Cordelia. This, when coupled with the negative actions of Amber, can foster a sense of dependency and codependence in the testator.

Finally, the Blum model:

1. <u>Isolation</u>: As mentioned already, evidence points to the fact that Amber worked to isolate Cordelia from others and especially from Flora.

2. <u>Dependency</u>: As mentioned already, Cordelia was almost completely dependent on Amber for her survival and care.

3. <u>Emotional Manipulation</u>: Here is a strike against undue influence. Amber may have been manipulating her mother's emotions, but I saw no evidence of it.

4. Exploitation of a Weakness: This did appear to occur. Amber likely would not have been able to write a lease termination letter to Flora or to solely dictate the terms of a new will had it not been for Cordelia's inability to think clearly, her inability to communicate, and her complete dependence on Amber.

5. Acquiescence: Cordelia acquiesced and signed the 2002 will. However, it is impossible to know if she read the will prior to signing it or whether she knew of its contents. We do, however, know that Amber fed Cordelia misinformation with inaccurate and deceptive complaints against Flora. It could very well be that

Cordelia grew to hate Flora as much as Amber did.

6. <u>Loss</u>: As mentioned before, Cordelia's estate plan ended up being vastly and shockingly different from her decades-long wish to treat her daughters equally.

So, there you go. That is a rough approximation of how a forensic expert might review the evidence and interpret it considering the leading psychological research and theory on undue influence. As mentioned before, my analysis is skewed by the fact that I knew the outcome of the case before my analysis, and publicly available write-ups of the case tended to focus on the evidence that pointed toward undue influence. I tried to find some evidence that might point away from undue influence, and I did in fact, find some.

In a typical case, even when I opine that undue influence occurred, there is typically more evidence pointing away from undue influence than I was able to find in the Doe case. It is the standard of practice for forensic experts to evaluate all plausible hypotheses (e.g., undue influence occurred! Or, no, undue influence didn't occur!). There will always be some amount of evidence that points toward undue influence and some amount of evidence that points away. When forming opinions, forensic experts must not ignore the evidence that is counter to their opinion; rather, they must acknowledge it and explain why that

evidence was not powerful enough to
change their opinion.

Next up: the end.

Chapter 17: The end

We know how the legal case ended for the Doe sisters, Amber and Flora. The will was overturned, Amber got her comeuppance, and the feuding sisters became co-owners of a lovely ranch.

We don't know what their relationship is like now, or if it survived the legal morass. I'm sure you have your guesses. I wish them well, and I hope they were able to find peace with one another.

And that's it. That's undue influence, minus all the sadness and human strife. I presented information on how the legal system views undue influence, and I highlighted how forensic experts understand the legal underpinnings of undue influence, review the evidence, and analyze that evidence using multiple research-based psychological models.

I picked the Doe case to highlight in this book because there was so much evidence pointing toward undue influence that it was easy for me to apply the psychological and legal theories to the facts to show you how it's done.

Juan, Cordelia, Amber, and Flora are unusual though. Typically, there is less one-sided evidence with which to work. Remember, you only need a preponderance of evidence to prove undue influence, and sometimes

51% is all an attorney can get to. On the flipside, sometimes all an attorney can eke out is 51% of the evidence to defend their case. It's messy, but it works. Those messy cases make for more confusing case studies though, and I wanted to keep it simple for this primer.

I also wanted the book to be brief, entertaining, accessible, and educational. After introducing the Doe family, I covered the legal concepts and psychological theories underlying undue influence. Using the Doe case as a guide, I showed how lawyers and forensic psychologists build the case for undue influence (or the lack thereof). Along the way, I provided definitions and explanations of some basic legal concepts for those who were previously unfamiliar.

If you're still here, reading these sentences, I appreciate you allowing me to take some of your valuable time to share with you what I know about undue influence. I am passionate about it, and I'm glad you found it interesting enough to stick through to the very end.

And as I end every one of my expert reports:

Respectfully submitted,

Max Wachtel, Ph.D.

About

Max Wachtel is a psychologist, licensed in Colorado and Wyoming. He is PSYPACT approved to conduct forensic evaluations in 41 states across the country.[33] At this point in his

---

[33] PSYPACT is an interstate compact that offers a voluntary expedited pathway for practice to qualified psychologists who wish to practice in multiple states. PSYPACT is designed to facilitate the practice of temporary, in-person, face-to-face psychology services such as forensic evaluations across state lines. Being PSYPACT approved does not imply an advanced skill, licensure, or education level. More information regarding PSYPACT and its requirements can be found at www.psypact.org.

career, he has conducted evaluations in twenty-two states.

He earned his bachelor's degree in 1995 from Trinity University, double majoring in psychology and religious studies. He has master's and doctoral degrees in counseling psychology from the University of Denver (1997 and 2001, respectively), and he has engaged in hundreds of hours of postgraduate training in forensic psychology,[34]

---

[34] The *APA Dictionary of Psychology, Second Edition (2015)* defines *forensic psychology* as "the application of psychological principles and techniques to situations involving the civil and criminal legal system."

forensic assessment,[35] geropsychology,[36] and neuropsychology.[37]

Since 2004, he has owned his own practice, where he specializes in forensic evaluation and assessment. Roughly 50% of his practice is clinical, where he works with, evaluates, and/or treats older individuals. About 25% of his practice involves

---

[35] APA (2015) defines *forensic assessment* as the "systematic evaluation by a mental health practitioner of a defendant, witness, or other offender for the purpose of informing the court about such issues as competency to stand trial, criminal responsibility, and risk assessment."

[36] APA (2015) defines *geropsychology* as "a specialization in psychology dealing with enhancing the welfare and mental health of older adults via the provision of various psychological services."

[37] *APA (2015)* defines *neuropsychology* as "the branch of science that studies the physiological processes of the nervous system and relates them to behavior and cognition, in terms both of their normal function and of the dysfunctional processes associated with brain damage."

conducting analyses where the individual in question is deceased. The remainder of his practice involves working with criminal defendants and civil litigants.

At this point in his career, he has conducted more than 2,000 evaluations. He has conducted more than 100 evaluations of testamentary and contractual capacity and undue influence.

He has presented multiple times on issues related to guardianship, conservatorship, will contests, testamentary capacity, contractual capacity, capacity to direct counsel, and undue influence. Many of these presentations qualified as Continuing Legal Education for elder law attorneys.

He has testified under oath more than 115 times, for both plaintiffs (and/or petitioners) and defendants (and/or respondents), and he has never failed to have been qualified as an expert. He has been qualified as an expert in both the legal and psychological aspects of undue influence and has been allowed to present opinion testimony on undue influence law to courts in multiple states.

In addition to his private practice, he was on the faculty of the University of Denver for 12 years, where he taught graduate level classes in psychological assessment, cognitive and neuropsychological assessment, and in the ethical and legal practice of psychology.

He has written four books, and he has studied and written about undue influence statutes and case law in all 50 states.[38]

He lives in Denver, Colorado with his wife, children, and dogs. He can be found running in his neighborhood and reading murder mysteries, often at the same time.

Learn more at www.maxwachtel.com, or email at max@maxwachtel.com.

---

[38] For more information, see www.maxwachtel.com/undue-influence.

Acknowledgements

I would like to thank Kim, my wife and business manager. Without her, I would not have my practice, and this book certainly would not exist. Thanks, Kim!

I'd like to thank my good friends, Myke Cole, Aki Peritz, and Connie Min, for reading early drafts of this book. Your daily support keeps me going.

My kids are a constant source of inspiration for me. I love you two goofballs!

My mom, dad, and sister have been a constant positive in my life, and I wouldn't be who I am without them.

Finally, Frank and Artemis, you are the best dogs ever.

www.ingramcontent.com/pod-product-compliance
Lightning Source LLC
Chambersburg PA
CBHW031434270326
41930CB00007B/694